Dear future revolutionaries,

Each generation can step into the future with all the discoveries of the generations before it. Let us learn the revolution from the greatest revolutionaries in world history.

This book contains 100 guidelines for a new revolution that future revolutionaries can learn from the wisdom of the generations before them. Each page contains a revolutionary guideline and a person from whom we learned it.

At the end of the book, all 100 guidelines come together to form a Revolutionary Manifesto - unified wisdom that the greatest revolutionaries pass on to future generations.

It's time. It's time for a revolution.

1. **First, dream. Then find strength. Patience. Passion. Now you are ready.**

Learned from Harriet Tubman (1820-1913), American abolitionist and political activist.[1]

---

[1] *»Every great dream begins with a dreamer. Always remember, you have within you the strength, the patience, and the passion to reach for the stars to change the world.« (Harriet Tubman)*

2. **If you do nothing, you may think you are free. Try it. Act.**

Learned from Rosa Luxemburg (1871-1919), Polish revolutionary socialist.[2]

---

[2] »*Those who do not move, do not notice their chains*« *(Rosa Luxemburg)*

3. **Freedom is no less than man's right to make sovereign decisions on all matters affecting his life.**

Learned from Josip Broz Tito (1892-1980), Yugoslav revolutionary, the leader of the Partisans and the President of Yugoslavia from 1953 to 1980.[3]

---

[3] *»Man's freedom consists not only in his right to freely express his opinions and aspirations but above all in his right and opportunities to make sovereign decisions on all matters concerning his life. « (Josip Broz Tito)*

4. Your mind is your most powerful oppressor.

Learned from Steve Biko (1946-1977), South African anti-apartheid activist.[4]

---

[4] *»The most potent weapon of the oppressor is the mind of the oppressed. « (Steve Biko)*

5. **Stop falling for everything and stand up for something.**

Learned from Rosa Parks (1913–2005), American activist in the civil rights movement.[5]

---

[5] *»Stand for something or you will fall for anything. Today's mighty oak is yesterday's nut that held its ground. « (Rosa Parks)*

6. **There is no happiness without following your conscience.**

Learned from George Washington (1732-1799), American political leader, general, founding father, and first president of the United States. [6]

---

[6] *»Human happiness and moral duty are inseparably connected. « (George Washington)*

7. **Open your eyes.**

Learned from Maya Angelou (1928-2014), American poet and civil right activist. [7]

---

[7] » We are only as blind as we want to be. « (Maya Angelou)

8. **Never be afraid to tell the truth.**

Learned from Rosa Luxemburg (1871-1919), Polish revolutionary socialist.[8]

---

[8] *»The most revolutionary thing one can do is always to proclaim loudly what is happening.« (Rosa Luxemburg)*

9. Choose your words carefully.

Learned from Abdelkader El Djezairi (1808-1883), Algerian leader who led a struggle against the French colonial invasion. [9]

---

[9] *»It is with a word as with an arrow-once let it loose and it does not return. « (Abdelkader El Djezairi)*

10.   There is no radical or conservative. It is only about right and wrong! Learned from Martin Luther King Jr. (1929-1968), American activist and leader in the civil rights movement. [10]

---

[10] »When you are right you cannot be too radical; when you are wrong, you cannot be too conservative« (Martin Luther King Jr.)

11.   Speak up! Silence
about things that matter
means dying slowly.

Learned from Martin Luther King
Jr. (1929-1968), American activist
and leader in the civil rights
movement. [11]

---

[11] *»Our lives begin to end the day we become silent about things that matter. « (Martin Luther King Jr.)*

12.   Passivity means acceptance. To accept evil is evil.

Learned from Martin Luther King Jr. (1929-1968), American activist and leader in the civil rights movement. [12]

---

[12] *»He who passively accepts evil is as much involved in it as he who helps to perpetrate it. He who accepts evil without protesting against it is really cooperating with it.« (Martin Luther King Jr.*

13.   **To face the truth can lead to despair. Desperation is a sign of a lack of education.**

Learned from Vladimir Lenin (1870-1924), a Russian revolutionary, political theorist, and a leader of the Soviet Union from 1922 to 1924.[13]

---

[13] *»Despair is typical of those who do not understand the causes of evil, see no way out, and are incapable of struggle.« (Vladimir Lenin)*

14.   **Educate yourself.**

Learned from Ernesto »Che« Guevara (1928-1967), an Argentine revolutionary, military theorist, guerilla leader, and a major figure of the Cuban Revolution.[14]

---

[14] *»The first duty of a revolutionary is to be educated.« (Che Guevara)*

15.   Do not learn the facts. Study to understand.

Learned from Ella Baker (1903-1986), American activist in the civil rights movement.[15]

---

[15] »In order to see where we are going, we not only must remember where we have been, but we must understand where we have been« (Ella Baker).

16.   Think for yourself!

Learned from Jose Marti (1853-1895), a Cuban revolutionary philosopher and political theorist.[16]

---

[16] *»The first duty of a man is to think for himself.«*

(Jose Marti)

17.   Follow the food chain and you will find your oppressor.

Learned from Thomas Sankara (1949-1987), Burkinabé revolutionary and president of Burkina Faso from 1983 to 1987.[17]

---

[17] *»He who feeds you, controls you. « (Thomas Sankara)*

18. Let history be your main teacher.

Learned from Sukarno (1901-1970), an Indonesian leader of the Indonesian struggle for independence from the Dutch Empire and the first president of Indonesia from 1945 to 1967.[18]

---

[18] »Never, ever forget history. Let us not be bitter about the past, but let us keep our eyes firmly on the future.« (Sukarno)

19. Develop a revolutionary theory.

Learned from Vladimir Lenin (1870-1924), a Russian revolutionary, political theorist, and a leader of the Soviet Union from 1922 to 1924.[19]

---

[19] *»Without a revolutionary theory there cannot be a revolutionary movement.« (Vladimir Lenin)*

20. **Learn from others so you can educate them.**

Learned from Mao Zedong (1893-1976), a Chinese revolutionary, the founding father of the People's Republic of China, and its leader from 1949 to 1976.[20]

---

[20] *»Learn from the masses, and then teach them.«* *(Mao Zedong)*

21. **Educate others. Ignorance is the secret of tyranny.**

Learned from Maximilien Robespierre (1758-1794), a French revolutionary, statesman, and one of the best-known and most influental figures of the French Revolution.[21]

---

[21] *»The secret of freedom lies in educating people, whereas the secret of tyranny is in keeping them ignorant.« (Maximilien Robespierre)*

22.   **Teach others to learn.**

Learned from Mao Zedong (1893-1976), a Chinese revolutionary, the founding father of the People's Republic of China, and its leader from 1949 to 1976.[22]

-----

[22] *»Don't give a child a fish but show him how to fish.«*
(Mao Zedong)

23.   **Be careful. Do not underestimate the fear of freedom.**

Learned from Jose Marti (1853-1895), a Cuban revolutionary philosopher and political theorist.[23]

---

[23] »It is terrible to speak of you, Liberty, for one who lives without you. « (Jose Marti)

24.   **Ignorance can be overcome.**

Learned from Malcolm X (1925-1965), an American human rights activist.[24]

---

[24] *»There was a time when you didn't know what you know today.« (Malcolm X)*

25.   **Once you have learned your theory, it is time to act.**

Learned from Karl Marx (1818-1883), a German philosopher, economist, political theorist, and socialist revolutionary. [25]

---

[25] *»The philosophers have only interpreted the world, in various ways. The point, however, is to change it.« (Karl Marx)*

26.   Security is a privilege. Earn it by fighting for freedom.

Learned from Benjamin Franklin (1706-1790), an American activist, political philosopher, statesman and one of the Founding Fathers of the United States. [26]

---

[26] *»They who can give up essential liberty to obtain a little temporary safety deserve neither liberty nor safety. « (Benjamin Franklin)*

27.   The revolution will not come of itself. It must be started.

Learned from Ernesto »Che« Guevara (1928-1967), an Argentine revolutionary, military theorist, guerilla leader, and a major figure of the Cuban Revolution.[27]

---

[27] *»The revolution is not an apple that falls when it is ripe. You have to make it fall.« (Che Guevara)*

28. Every revolution begins with an idea.

Learned from Agostinho Neto (1922-1979), Angolan politician, leader of the Popular Movement fort he Liberation of Angola in the war for independence, and the first president of Angola from 1975-1979.[28]

---

[28] *»A silent idea is louder than spoken words. «*
(Agostinho Neto)

29.   The revolution necessarily arises from the *status quo* before the revolution.

Learned from Leon Trotsky (1879-1940), a Russian revolutionary, political theorist and politician.[29]

---

[29] »The dynamic of revolutionary events is directly determined by swift, intense, and passionate changes in the psychology of classes which have already formed themselves before the revolution. « (Leon Trotsky)

30. **Anyone can change the world. Yes, even you.**

Learned from Ernesto »Che« Guevara (1928-1967), an Argentine revolutionary, military theorist, guerilla leader, and a major figure of the Cuban Revolution.[30]

---

[30] *»You can change the world.« (Che Guevara)*

31. **Do not make predictions. Make the future.**

Learned from Abraham Lincoln (1809-1865), an American statesman that succeeded in abolishing slavery and the 16th president of the United States from 1861-1865.[31]

---

[31] *»The best way to predict your future is to create it. « (Abraham Lincoln)*

32.   Take fate into your own hands!

Learned from Gamal Abdel Nasser (1918-1970), Egyptian politician who led the 1952 overthrow of the monarchy and the second president of Egypt from 1956 to 1970.[32]

---

[32] *»Fate does not jest, and events are not a matter of chance. There is no existence out of nothing.«*
(Gamal Abdel Nasser)

33.   **Nothing is impossible.**

Learned by Nelson Mandela (1918-2013), a South African anti-apartheid revolutionary and political leader who served as president of South Africa from 1994 to 1999.[33]

---

[33] »It always seems impossible until it's done.« (Nelson Mandela)

34.   **No excuses!**

Learned from George Washington (1732-1799), an American political leader, general, and a founding father who served as the first president of the United States. [34]

---

[34] »99% of failures come from people who make excuses.« (George Washington)

35. The time is always right!

Learned from Martin Luther King Jr. (1929-1968), American activist and leader in the civil rights movement. [35]

---

[35] *»Don t wait for the right time. The time is always right to do what is right. « (Martin Luther King Jr.)*

36.   Tomorrow is too late.

Learned from Benjamin Franklin
(1706-1790), an American activist,
political philosopher, statesman
and one of the Founding Fathers of
the United States. [36]

---

[36] *»Never leave that till tomorrow which you can do today.« (Benjamin Franklin)*

37.   Fight against the oppressors. The oppressors will never agree to the freedom of the oppressed.

Learned from Jean-Paul Marat (1743-1793), a French political theorist and revolutionary.[37]

---

[37] *»It is the height of stupidity to claim that men who for a thousand years have had the power to berate us, to fleece us and to oppress us with impunity, will now agree, with good grace, to be our equals.«*
(Jean-Paul Marat)

38.   For some, the *status quo* means security.

Learned from Martin Luther King Jr. (1929-1968), American activist and leader in the civil rights movement. [38]

---

[38] »The soft-minded man always fears change. He feels security in the status quo, and he has an almost morbid fear of the new. For him, the greatest pain is the pain of a new idea. « (Martin Luther King Jr.)

39. **No one will give you freedom. Demand it!**

Learned from Martin Luther King Jr. (1929-1968), American activist and leader in the civil rights movement. [39]

---

[39] *»Freedom is never voluntarily given by the oppressor; it must be demanded by the oppressed. « (Martin Luther King Jr)*

40. Only the struggle can stop the humiliation.

Learned from Emiliano Zapata (1879-1919), a Mexican revolutionary, the main leader of the peasant revolution in the state of Morelos, and the inspiration of the agrarian movement called *Zapatismo*.[40]

---

[40] *»It is better to die on your feet than to live on your knees. « (Emiliano Zapata)*

41. For the future, you fight the past.

Learned from Fidel Castro (1926-2016), a Cuban revolutionary, the leader of Cuban revolution who served as prime Minister of Cuba from 1959 to 1976 and president of Cuba drom 1976 to 2008.[41]

---

[41] *»A revolution is not a bed of roses. A revolution is a struggle to the death between the future and the past.« (Fidel Castro)*

42.   Be a man of the future, fighting for the future!

Learned from Mustafa Kemal Ataturk (1881-1938), a Turkish field marshal, revolutionary statesman and the founding father of the Republic of Turkey, who served as the president of Turkey from 1923 to 1938.[42]

---

[42] *»Do you want to be a man of today or a man of tomorrow?« (Mustafa Kemal Ataturk)*

43.   There is no freedom without struggle.

Learned from Ernesto »Che« Guevara (1928-1967), an Argentine revolutionary, military theorist, guerilla leader, and a major figure of the Cuban Revolution.[43]

---

[43] *»We have no right to believe that freedom can be won without struggle. « (Che Guevara)*

44.   The fight for freedom always means breaking the rules.

Learned from Maximilien Robespierre (1758-1794), a French revolutionary, statesman, and one of the best-known and most influental figures of the French Revolution.[44]

---

[44] *»You can't make an omelet without breaking a few eggs. « (Maximilien Robespierre)*

45. The right to fight tyranny is above the law.

Learned from Simón Bolívar (1783-1830), a Venezuelan revolutionary and liberator who led what are currently the countries of Venezuela, Bolivia, Colombia, Ecuador, Peru and Panama to independence from the Spanish Empire.[45]

---

[45] *»When tyranny becomes law, rebellion is a right.«*
(Simón Bolívar)

46.   Revolution is not domination. Revolution is about change.

Learned from Jose Mujica (1935), a Uruguayan politician who served as the 40th president of Uruguay from 2010 to 2015.[46]

---

[46] »The world will always need revolution. That doesn't mean shooting and violence. A revolution is when you change your thinking. « (Jose Mujica)

47.   Revolution is not about pretty phrases and slogans. It's about changing reality.

Learned from Thomas Sankara (1949-1987), Burkinabé revolutionary and president of Burkina Faso from 1983 to 1987.[47]

---

[47] *»Our revolution is not a battle of fine phrases. Our revolution is, and should continue to be, the collective effort of revolutionaries to transform reality, to improve the concrete situation of the masses of our country.« (Thomas Sankara)*

48.   You have to put an idea behind every word.

Learned from Léopold Sédar Senghor (1906-2001), a Senegalese politician and cultural theorist who served as the first president of Senegal drom 1960 to 1980. [48]

---

[48] »I have always taken care to put an idea or emotion behind my words. I have made it a habit to be suspicious of the mere music of words. « (Léopold Sédar Senghor)

49.   **Do not be a lunatic. Make sure that everybody takes you seriously.**

Learned from Steve Biko (1946-1977), South African anti-apartheid activist.[49]

---

[49] »If you want to say something radical, you should dress conservative. « (Steve Biko)

50.　**Always be prepared. Always have a plan.**

Learned from Fidel Castro (1926-2016), a Cuban revolutionary, the leader of Cuban revolution who served as prime minister of Cuba from 1959 to 1976 and president of Cuba from 1976 to 2008.[50]

____

[50] »It does not matter how small you are if you have faith and a plan of action. « (Fidel Castro)

51.   There are no easy ways.

Learned from Ernesto »Che« Guevara (1928-1967), an Argentine revolutionary, military theorist, guerilla leader, and a major figure of the Cuban Revolution.[51]

---

[51] *»If you can find ways without any obstacles, it probably leads nowhere. « (Che Guevara)*

52. **Do not be afraid to be afraid. Fight the fear.**

Learned by Nelson Mandela (1918-2013), a South African anti-apartheid revolutionary and political leader who served as president of South Africa from 1994 to 1999.[52]

---

[52] *»I learned that courage was not the absence of fear, but the triumph over it. The brave man is not he who does not feel afraid, but he who conquers that fear« (Nelson Mandela)*

53.   Dare!

Learned from George–Jacques Danton (1759-1794), a French revolutionary and a leading figure in the early stages of the French revolution.[53]

---

[53] »We must dare, and dare again, and go on daring.« (George-Jacques Danton)

54. **Determination overcomes fear.**

Learned from Rosa Parks (1913–2005), American activist in the civil rights movement.[54]

---

[54] »I have learned over the years that when one's mind is made up, this diminishes fear; knowing what must be done does away with fear. « (Rosa Parks)

55.   There is no perfect way.

Learned from Patrice Lumumba, a Congolese politician and independence leader who played a significant role in transformation of Congo drom a colony of Belgium into an independent republic.[55]

---

[55] »No one is perfect in this imperfect world.« (Patrice Lumumba)

56.   Everyone has the right to make a mistake.

Learned from Mahatma Gandhi (1869-1948), an Indian lawyer, who employed nonviolent resistance to lead the successful campaign for India's independence.[56]

---

[56] *»Freedom is not worth having if it does not include the freedom to make mistakes.« (Mahatma Gandhi)*

57. **Let your principles guide you. Never betray them.**

Learned from Emiliano Zapata (1879-1919), a Mexican revolutionary, the main leader of the peasant revolution in the state of Morelos, and the inspiration of the agrarian movement called *Zapatismo.*[57]

---

[57] *»I want to die as a slave to principles, not to men. «*
(Emiliano Zapata)

58.   **The revolutionary must always have compassion fort the oppressed.**

Learned from Ernesto »Che« Guevara (1928-1967), an Argentine revolutionary, military theorist, guerilla leader, and a major figure of the Cuban Revolution.[58]

---

[58] *»Above all, try to be able to feel deeply any injustice committed against any person in any part of the world. « (Che Guevara)*

59.   Men and women are equal in the revolution.

Learned from Thomas Sankara (1949-1987), Burkinabé revolutionary and president of Burkina Faso from 1983 to 1987.[59]

---

[59] *»May my eyes never see and my feet never take me to a society where half the people are held in silence. I hear the roar of women's silence. I sense the rumble of their storm and feel the fury of their revolt. « (Thomas Sankara)*

60. **If women are not equal to men, the essential task of the revolution is to make them equal.**

Learned from Samora Machel (1933-1986), a Mozambican revolutionary and a politician who served as the first president of Mozambique from 1975 to 1986.[60]

---

[60] *»The liberation of women is a fundamental necessity for the revolution, a guarantee of its continuity and a precondition for its victory. «* (Samora Machel)

61.   **The revolutionary body must be united.**

Learned from Martin Luther King Jr. (1929-1968), American activist and leader in the civil rights movement. [61]

---

[61] *»We may all come on different ships, but we're in the same boat now. « (Martin Luther King Jr.)*

62.   **Only whose who are willing to give everything for freedom deserve to be free.**

Learned from Malcolm X (1925-1965), an American human rights activist.[62]

____

[62] »If you're not ready to die for it, put the word 'freedom' out of your vocabulary. « (Malcolm X)

63.　Leading means risking everything.

Learned by Nelson Mandela (1918-2013), a South African anti-apartheid revolutionary and political leader who served as president of South Africa from 1994 to 1999.[63]

---

[63] *»Real leaders must be ready to sacrifice all for the freedom of their people.« (Nelson Mandela)*

64.   **Do not try to be a strong leader. Try to make the people around you stronger.**

Learned from Ella Baker (1903-1986), American activist in the civil rights movement.[64]

---

[64] *»Strong people do not need strong leaders.« (Ella Baker)*

65.   There is no greater force than the force of people.

Learned from Mao Zedong (1893-1976), a Chinese revolutionary, the founding father of the People's Republic of China, and its leader from 1949 to 1976.[65]

---

[65] *»The people, and the people alone, are the motive force in the making of world history.« (Mao Zedong)*

66.   Guide. Do not push.

Learned from Ella Baker (1903-1986), American activist in the civil rights movement.[66]

---

[66] *»Give light, and people will find the way...« (Ella Baker)*

67.   **Do not complicate.
Make everyone
understand.**

Learned from Ho Chi Minh (1890-
1969), a Vietnamese revolutionary
and politician, who served as
prime minister of Vietnam from
1945 to 1955 and president from
1945 to 1969.[67]

---

[67] *»Write in such a way as that you can be readily understood by both the young and the old, by men as well as women, even by children.« (Ho Chi Minh)*

**68.   Do not be arrogant.
Always be ready to listen.**

Learned from José de San Martín
(1778-1850), an Argentine general
and the prime leader of the
southern and central parts of
South America's successful
struggle for independence from
Spanish Empire, who served as the
Protector of Peru.[68]

------

[68] *»My best friend is he who rights my wrongs or
reproaches my mistakes.« (José de San Martín)*

69.   Try to understand the irrational.

Learned by Nelson Mandela (1918-2013), a South African anti-apartheid revolutionary and political leader who served as president of South Africa from 1994 to 1999.[69]

---

[69] *»If you talk to a man in a language he understands, that goes to his head. If you talk to him in his language, that goes to his heart. « (Nelson Mandela)*

70.   **Make every revolutionary who participates important.**

Learned by Nelson Mandela (1918-2013), a South African anti-apartheid revolutionary and political leader who served as president of South Africa from 1994 to 1999.[70]

---

[70] *»Lead from the back — and let others believe they are in front. « (Nelson Mandela)*

71.   In revolution, every person counts

Learned from Josip Broz Tito (1892-1980), Yugoslav revolutionary, the leader of the Partisans and the President of Yugoslavia from 1953 to 1980.[71]

---

[71] *»One should not always look only at the masses, but one should see each individual, one should see, feel, understand the difficulties that the individual is facing, one should try to help him, and he must be helped. (Josip Broz Tito)*

72. **Measure each person in times of challenge and controversy.**

Learned from Martin Luther King Jr. (1929-1968), American activist and leader in the civil rights movement. [72]

---

[72] *»The ultimate measure of a man is not where he stands in moments of comfort and convenience, but where he stands at times of challenge and controversy. « (Martin Luther King Jr.)*

73.	**Let your conscience judge you.**

Learned from José de San Martín (1778-1850), an Argentine general and the prime leader of the southern and central parts of South America's successful struggle for independence from Spanish Empire, who served as the Protector of Peru.[73]

---

[73] »»The conscience is the best and most impartial judge that a righteous man has. « (José de San Martín)

74.   Not giving up is the key to victory.

Learned by Nelson Mandela (1918-2013), a South African anti-apartheid revolutionary and political leader who served as president of South Africa from 1994 to 1999.[74]

---

[74] »A winner is a dreamer who never gives up.« (Nelson Mandela)

75. **Your will is your power.**

Learned from Mahatma Gandhi (1869-1948), an Indian lawyer, who employed nonviolent resistance to lead the successful campaign for India's independence.[75]

____

[75] *»Strength does not come from physical capacity. It comes from an indomitable will.« (Mahatma Gandhi)*

76.   **Do not give up. Do what you can.**

Learned from Martin Luther King Jr. (1929-1968), American activist and leader in the civil rights movement. [76]

---

[76] »If you can't fly then run, if you can't run then walk, if you can't walk then crawl, but whatever you do you have to keep moving forward.« (Martin Luther King Jr.)

77.   Do your best and nothing less.

Learned from Jose Marti (1853-1895), a Cuban revolutionary philosopher and political theorist.[77]

---

[77] - »It is a sin not to do what one is capable of doing.« (Jose Marti)

78.   **Do not settle for small victories.**

Learned from Karl Marx (1818-1883), a German philosopher, economist, political theorist, and socialist revolutionary. [78]

---

[78] *»The rich will do anything for the poor but get off their backs. « (Karl Marx)*

79. **Never stop. Keep on fighting.**

Learned from Huey P. Newton (1942-1989), an American revolutionary and political activist, who co-founded the Black Panther Party.[79]

---

[79] *»If you stop struggling, then you stop life. « (Huey P. Newton)*

80.   **Jails cannot stop the revolution.**

Learned from Huey P. Newton (1942-1989), an American revolutionary and political activist, who co-founded the Black Panther Party.[80]

---

[80] - »You can jail a Revolutionary, but you can't jail the Revolution. « (Huey P. Newton)

81. **Every defeat is a
lesson for the next time.**

Learned from Malcolm X (1925-
1965), an American human rights
activist.[81]

---

[81] *»Every defeat, every heartbreak, every loss,
contains its own seed, its own lesson on how to
improve your performance next time. « (Malcolm X)*

82. **The harder you fight, the more glorious your victory will be.**

Learned from Thomas Paine (1737-1809), an American revolutionary, political activist, philosopher and political theorist.[82]

---

[82] *»The harder the conflict, the more glorious the triumph.» (Thomas Paine)*

83. **Victory may come after your time.**

Learned from Ernesto »Che« Guevara (1928-1967), an Argentine revolutionary, military theorist, guerilla leader, and a major figure of the Cuban Revolution.[83]

---

[83] *»I have a wish. It is a fear as well – that in my end will be my beginning. « (Che Guevara)*

84.   **Every man is mortal.
An idea is not.**

Learned from Thomas Sankara
(1949-1987), Burkinabé
revolutionary and president of
Burkina Faso from 1983 to 1987.[84]

---

[84] *»While revolutionaries as individuals can be murdered, you cannot kill ideas.« (Thomas Sankara)*

85. **Nothing can hold down the idea of the people. The revolution will win.**

Learned from Huey P. Newton (1942-1989), an American revolutionary and political activist, who co-founded the Black Panther Party.[85]

---

[85] *»The walls, the bars, the guns and the guards can never encircle or hold down the idea of the people. « (Huey Newton)*

86.   After the revolution the hardest work begins.

Learned by Nelson Mandela (1918-2013), a South African anti-apartheid revolutionary and political leader who served as president of South Africa from 1994 to 1999.[86]

---

[86] *»After climbing a great hill. One only finds that there are many more hills to climb.« (Nelson Mandela)*

87. **A successful revolution is never the end. Every revolution must constantly evolve and defend its heritage.**

Learned from Josip Broz Tito (1892-1980), Yugoslav revolutionary, the leader of the Partisans and the President of Yugoslavia from 1953 to 1980.[87]

---

[87] *»Every revolution is worth as much as it is able to constantly develop and defend its achievements!«*
(Josip Broz Tito)

88. **Be optimistic, look to the future, but be prepared, as if the struggle continues tomorrow.**

Learned from Josip Broz Tito (1892-1980), Yugoslav revolutionary, the leader of the Partisans and the President of Yugoslavia from 1953 to 1980.[88]

---

[88] *»We work as if we would live 100 years, we prepare as if there would be a war tomorrow. « (Josip Broz Tito)*

89.   **Do not allow your revolution to be stolen.**

Learned from the Arab spring revolutionaries from Tunisia, Libya, Egypt and Syria.[89]

---

[89]   »They stole the Revolution from us.« (Revolutionaries from Tunisia, Libya, Egypt and Syria)

90. **Be humble. The success of the revolution is not your success.**

Learned from Mustafa Kemal Ataturk (1881-1938), a Turkish field marshal, revolutionary statesman and the founding father of the Republic of Turkey, who served as the president of Turkey from 1923 to 1938.[90]

---

[90] *»The happiest ones are those who have a character which would prefer their services to be unknown to all generations. « (Mustafa Kemal Ataturk)*

91. **Do not become what you fought against.**

Learned from Abraham Lincoln (1809-1865), an American statesman that succeeded in abolishing slavery and the 16th president of the United States from 1861-1865.[91]

---

[91] *»Nearly all men can stand adversity, but if you want to test a man's character, give him power. «* *(Abraham Lincoln)*

92.   **Do not use the old unjust procedures from pre-revolutionary times to achieve revolutionary goals.**

Learned from Lucía Sánchez Saornil (1895-1970), a Spanish revolutionary, poet and feminist.[92]

---

[92] *»New life must be built by new procedures. «
(Lucía Sánchez Saornil)*

93.   **Everything you have fought for can collapse in an instant. One foolish act is enough.**

Learned from Benjamin Franklin (1706-1790), an American activist, political philosopher, statesman and one of the Founding Fathers of the United States. [93]

---

[93] *»It takes many good deeds to build a good reputation, and only one bad one to lose it.«* *(Benjamin Franklin)*

94. **Remember that power is not a goal but a necessary evil.**

Learned from Thomas Paine (1737-1809), an American revolutionary, political activist, philosopher and political theorist.[94]

---

[94] *»Government, even in its best state, is but a necessary evil; in its worst state, an intolerable one. « (Thomas Paine)*

95. **Do not ask for too much. Do not give too little. Be righteous!**

Learned from Mikhail Bakunin (1814-1876), a Russian revolutionary anarchist and founder of collectivist anarchism.[95]

---

[95] *»From each according to his faculties; to each according to his needs.« (Mikhail Bakunin)*

96.   Be strong. Forgive!

Learned from Mahatma Gandhi (1869-1948), an Indian lawyer, who employed nonviolent resistance to lead the successful campaign for India's independence.[96]

---

[96] *»The weak can never forgive. Forgiveness is an attribute of the strong« (Mahatma Gandhi)*

97.   Simply act positively.

Learned from Gamal Abdel Nasser (1918-1970), Egyptian politician who led the 1952 overthrow of the monarchy and the second president of Egypt from 1956 to 1970.[97]

---

[97] *»Power is to act positively with all the components of power.« (Gamal Abdel Nasser)*

98.   **The revolution is not for those who take part in it. The revolution is for everyone.**

Learned from Jose Marti (1853-1895), a Cuban revolutionary philosopher and political theorist.[98]

---

[98] *»We light the oven so that everyone may bake bread in it. « (Jose Marti)*

_99._ **After the transition your work is done. It' s time to leave the power to the people.**

Learned from Mustafa Kemal Ataturk (1881-1938), a Turkish field marshal, revolutionary statesman and the founding father of the Republic of Turkey, who served as the president of Turkey from 1923 to 1938.[99]

---

[99] *»I will lead my people by the hand along the road until their feet are sure and they know the way. Then they may choose for themselves and rule themselves. Then my work will be done. « (Mustafa Kemal Ataturk)*

100.   History will decide whether the revolution was right.

Learned from Leon Trotsky (1879-1940), a Russian revolutionary, political theorist and politician.[100]

---

[100] *»The historic ascent of humanity, taken as a whole, may be summarized as a succession of victories of consciousness over blind forces - in nature, in society, in man himself. « (Leon Trotsky)*

The Revolutionary Manifesto

First, dream. Then find strength. Patience. Passion. Now you are ready.

If you do nothing, you may think you are free. Try it. Take action. Freedom is no less than man's right to make sovereign decisions on all matters affecting his life. Your mind is your most powerful oppressor. Stop falling for everything and stand up for something. There is no happiness without following your conscience. Open your eyes. Never be afraid to tell the truth. Choose your words carefully. There is no radical or conservative. It is only about right and wrong. Speak up! Silence about things that matter means dying slowly. Passivity means acceptance. To accept evil is evil.

To face the truth can lead to despair. Desperation is a sign of a lack of education. Educate yourself! Do not learn the facts. Study to understand. Think for yourself! Follow the food chain and you will find your oppressor. Let history be your main teacher. Develop a revolutionary theory. Learn from others so you can educate them. Educate others. Ignorance is the secret of tyranny. Teach others to learn. Be careful. Do not underestimate the fear of freedom. Ignorance can be overcome. Once you have learned your theory, it is time to act. Security is a privilege. Earn it by fighting for freedom.

The revolution will not come of itself. It must be started. Every revolution begins with an idea. The revolution necessarily arises from the status quo before the revolution. Anyone can change the world. Yes, even you. Make no predictions. Make the future. Take fate into your own hands! Nothing is impossible. No excuses! The time is always right! Tomorrow is too late. Fight against the oppressors. The oppressors will never agree to the freedom of the oppressed. For some, the status quo means security. No one will give you your freedom. Demand it! Only the struggle can stop the humiliation. Fight. For the future, you fight the past. Be a man of the future, fighting for the future!

There is no freedom without struggle. The fight for freedom always means breaking the rules. The right to fight tyranny is above the law. Revolution is not domination. Revolution is about change. Revolution is not about pretty phrases and slogans. It's about changing reality. You have to put an idea behind every word. Do not be a lunatic. Make sure that everybody takes you seriously. Always be prepared. Always have a plan. There are no easy ways. Do not be afraid to be afraid. Fight the fear. Dare! Determination overcomes fear. There is no perfect way. Everyone has the right to make a mistake. Let your principles guide you. Never betray them.

The revolutionary must always have compassion for the oppressed. Men and women are equal in the revolution. If women are not equal to men, the essential task of the revolution is to make them equal. The revolutionary body must be united. Only those who are willing to give everything for freedom deserve to be free.

Leading means risking everything. Do not try to be a strong leader. Try to make the people around you stronger. There is no greater force than the force of people. Guide. Do not push. Do not complicate. Make everyone understand. Do not be arrogant. Always be ready to listen. Try to understand the irrational. Make every revolutionary who participates important. In the revolution, every person counts. Measure each person in times of challenge and controversy. Let your conscience judge you.

Not giving up is the key to victory. Your will is your power. Do not give up. Do what you can. Do your best and nothing less. Do not settle for small victories. Never stop. Keep on fighting. Jails cannot stop the revolution. Every defeat is a lesson for the next time. The harder you fight, the more glorious your victory will be. Victory may come after your time. Every man is mortal. An idea is not. Nothing can hold down the idea of the people. The revolution will win.

After a successful revolution, the hardest work begins. A successful revolution is never the end. Every revolution must constantly evolve and defend its heritage. Be optimistic, look to the future, but be prepared, as if the struggle continues tomorrow. Do not allow your revolution to be stolen. Be humble. The success of the revolution is not your success.

Do not become what you fought against. Do not use the old unjust procedures from pre-revolutionary times to achieve revolutionary goals. Everything you have fought for can collapse in an instant. One foolish act is enough. Remember that power is not a goal, but a necessary evil. Do not ask for too much. Do not give too little. Be righteous! Be strong. Forgive! Simply act positively.

The revolution is not for those who participate in it. The revolution is for everyone. After the transition, your work is done. It' s time to hand over power to the people.

History will decide if the revolution was right.

United Revolutionary Forces of History